BAD KARMA FOR GOOD DEEDS

PART 1

YOU ARE NEVER ALONE

Donovan Broderick

ISBN: 978-1-7353610-7-9

Unless otherwise expressed, all quotations and references must be permitted by Authors. All scripture references from NKJ and NIV Bibles.

Cover Design:
Business Startup & Marketing Solutions LLC
and JWG Publishing House.

Published by

JWG Publishing
Printed in the United States of America.

DEDICATION
PAGE

This book is dedicated to my heaven sent mother, Corine Kameka, my source of strength. And also to my two beautiful daughters, they mean the world to me even when they get on top of my last nerve. They are both my reason for breathing, daddy love you both.

TABLE OF CONTENTS

ACKNOWLEDGEMENTS

I can't express enough thanks to my family and friends for their continued support and encouragement throughout the years, my loving mother, Corine Kameka and my brother Richard Broderick. Denessia Carr, Tracy-Ann Walker and Monique Graham, thank you.

The completion of this project would not have been accomplished without the support of my loving wife Michelle Sheppy Broderick. My deepest gratitude, my tower of strength when I am hopeless and when my back is against the wall.

My lighthouse when my path is dark. My speaker when I'm voiceless. For all that you have done, you are well appreciated, and it's duly noted. It was a great comfort and relief to know that you were willing to help me with ideas and insight to make this a success.

My heartfelt thanks.

INTRODUCTION

This book is guaranteed to change people's opinion and mind concerning poetry. Most people find poetry to be boring and most poets lack the ability to keep their reader engaged, well this book promises to change all that.

Every topic in this book will open up your mind to wanting more; the content will evoke emotions and stimulate thoughts. If you read this book to the end, I promise you that your whole outlook on poetry will be renewed; this book is a game changer. Why? Most of the content is based on real life situations, there's a topic for everyone, the poems are not just regular poems, they are stories of love, stories of toxic relationships, trauma, healing and overcoming these adversities.

This book was inspired by the good and bad of this world. It is without bias and stereotype. All are welcome to read, its food for the soul; feed on its knowledge to handle the challenges you'll face in this world of skepticism. This book is motivation gold, are you ready to read?

WHY I SWITCHED

All my life, I have been abused and used by men. I'm tired of it and I won't pretend. A friend of mine always encouraged me to get out of toxic relationships, my eyes black and blue with a swollen face and lips. I always ran to my friend's house to get away from my abusive spouse. Crying in her arms, while she's stroking my hair and telling me try to be calm.

I found comfort in her arms, a comfort I can't find in a male. Her words of motivation strengthened me and helped me to prevail. What changed everything is when she kissed me. I was shocked but for some reason, I kissed her back. I never thought I would be attracted to the same sex, but her touch eased my stress.

I was once beaten until I was unconscious. I woke up in the hospital with three broken ribs and an excruciating pain around my occipital. I told myself I hate men. I survived that ordeal, and the relationship came to an end. I have tried time and time again, but the same trend happens. I said to myself to hell with men! This abuse has to end.

I never expected another woman to bring me comfort. I never thought her kiss could make me forget about the hurt. I never thought I would crave a woman's touch at nights, I never thought I would need her reassurance that everything would be alright. She makes me smile again, my lover and best-friend.

I used to say same-sex attraction is twisted. I learned never to judge, all my life I have seen myself with a man. Look at me now, in the arms of a woman. She holds me down firmer than any man can. She keeps me focused and now it's all about us. Her gentle touch, my body can't get enough, I finally feel loved.

My best friend is now my lover, rock, strong tower and motivator. She believes in me more than I believe in myself. She's all I need and no one else, if I can't have her, I would rather be by myself. Love is a strange thing, it is gender blind. Strange enough, she is mine. Back then, I loving another woman would be strange like snow falling in the Caribbean.

SINS OF MY MIND

I have my wife, but that doesn't stop me from lusting every day. I try to focus, but I can't help staring at beautiful ladies passing my way. I have never cheated on my wife, but in my mind I did. Mentally, so many ladies I slept with, they passed me every day in clothes, but in my thoughts, they were all naked.

These gorgeous women have touched my life in so many ways without knowing. I'm so glad my thoughts weren't showing. I'm a faithful and trustworthy husband, but in my mind, I'm a womanizer and a man who finds it hard to stick to one woman. My wife is sweet and sexy, cuts out like a diamond, but in my mind, I thinking about the hips of a Spanish woman.

I love my wife so much, but in my mind, I crave someone else's touch. My wife means the world to me, but in my mind, I wish I was King Solomon, with 700 girls all for me. If my wife ever knew how much I lust, she would hit me with the Bible and tell me to read Leviticus. Ray Charles couldn't stick with one woman and he's blind, I have one and my eyes are quite fine.

A woman is the most precious gift to a man, but! I only can have one? So why didn't King Solomon and King David see themselves with only one? That's an interesting question. My wife is a nice Christian woman, but I wish we were Muslims, so I could also have Latoya and Kim.

I love my wife, and I will never hurt her. I respect even the mother who birthed her. All my sins are in my mind, to her, I'm upright and one of a kind. I complimented her every day, whatever I did wrong; only I and God can say, in my thoughts it will all stay. I'm a man, so I think like one; maybe she's not brave enough to let me know how she thinks as a woman.

It doesn't mean that I will go astray and disrespect a good woman. Monogamy is even rare among animals, Humans are classified as mammals. Questions in my head, one lady, one wife, one gal? I love my wife so I'm sticking with her and that's final.

PASTOR'S WIFE

I love my husband, a man who loves and fears God, but he spends all his time for the church and not for me, that's why I'm so mad. No cuddle time, he would rather talk about how Jesus turned the water into wine. I love him and I wouldn't trade him for fortune and fame, but he needs to remember that he has a wife to maintain.

What about me? I look beautiful by his side but what people don't know, I can't get his arms around me at night. He is always tired, and I can't even get a 15-minute ride. His favorite scripture is "Trust in the Lord with all your heart and lean not on your own understanding," well, there is something notwithstanding.

Every Sunday morning, we gather in church to give praise and thanks. My husband preaches, "Whoso findeth a wife findeth a good thing." Oh please! The only thing good is the ring! Physically, emotionally and sexually I'm suffering. He's always busy quoting, and I need a little squeeze and pampering.

I was a member of the choir when we met. He treated me like a queen back then, and I thought I would always have his heart. I wore a bright smile on my face whenever he used his rag to wipe my sweat, when he gets complacent? Has the Persian rug turned into a door mat? He thinks I'm a trophy or some kind of mascot.

I missed the man I fell in love with, not the preacher but my husband: my rock, the foundation on which I stand, my mighty tower of strength and my daily motivation. Does he know how long I haven't felt butterflies in my stomach around him? Instead, he has me hanging around like a hammock! That's my beautiful wife and beating his stomach.

I love the Lord and I'm a follower of the words in the Bible, but the way he treats me makes me wonder, if he reads the Bible from a different angle.

I love him, so I won't walk away. *Sigh*….

REINCARNATION

I t was a mutual attraction. The first time I laid eyes on her, I asked myself, *where have we met before?* I know we were meant to be together — of this, I'm sure. I saw her face before, maybe in another time and place. My eyes were familiar with her beauty. My mind remembered how tight she used to hold me.

She loved me once but not in this life, maybe she was once my wife. Her presence brings me peace of mind, maybe she was my comforter once upon a time. She gazed into my eyes and smiled, we were both speechless for a while. I finally found someone to whom I truly belong. I went over, "Hello, how do you do?" She replied, with a smile, "I'm fine and thank you."

"There is something about you," she said. "I feel the same way about you." It felt like a match made in heaven, I was supposed to be home by 7 p.m. but I got home at 11:00 p.m. I lost track of time. Listening to her angelic voice and gazing into her hazel eyes.

I can't wait for tomorrow to come. I know tomorrow is going to be fun. Tossing and turning in my bed, I can't get her out of my head. I have never believed in reincarnation, but I changed my views since I met this woman. Her hands fit mine perfectly; her smile touches the uttermost part of me. Her words will be doctrines I live by daily, I can't wait to see her in the morning bright and early.

The cock crows, yesterday is gone. Tomorrow was a promise, today is the day I look forward to. Before I even take a bath, I picked up my phone and dialed her number.

"Hi!"

"Good morning!"

"Question, what time will we be meeting?"

"Let's meet at nine. Will that time be fine?"

"Sure!"

I reached exactly 9 a.m., she was a minute late but she was worth the wait. She was elegantly dressed like an Arabian princess; I was dressed in all blue because that's my favorite hue. We hugged, I didn't want to let her go, and her body next to mine promises a better tomorrow. We spent the evening together, nothing matters as long as we have each other. It feels like she had my soul in her hands, Just by looking into her beautiful eyes put me in a trance. Each moment was well spent, I'm so grateful for this heaven-sent.

THE MAN
IN ME

I'm a girl but I don't feel like it, I like wearing Clarks and Reebok classic. Look like a boy in public, I like to wear pants, hang out with boys on the block and do street dance. I feel more masculine than feminine, hated skirt, I rather wear Jeans and T-shirt, wish I was a boy from birth.

My parents said I'm a disgrace to the family, nothing about me is girly, I wore boy clothing and I walked manly. I have a girl voice but it isn't sexy, I wear boxers, I can't see myself wearing panties. I have a female face and body but I think like a male, it's my life I have no need to give anyone my personal details.

I love the company of men, I have a male as my best-friend nothing intimate we are just friends. My male friends treated me more like a little brother than a little sister; I wore a close fitted bra to keep my chest flat. I look like another boy on the block, "Timberland and baggy Jeans", Snapback Hat.

It is my life, why my parents telling me how to live it? Telling everybody about how your daughter loves wearing male outfits. I was born like this, I hate when people dictate to me about female practices. Don't tell me how to live my life, which will get me pissed; I am dressing up like a man has nothing to do with neither inequality nor being a feminist.

I just want to live my life and feel free to make my own decisions without any interference; this is my life and my side of the fence. Only God can judge me, nothing that all of you say budged me. For every woman out there like me, be you and let no one define who you are, be true to you.

THE CHILD IS NOT MINE

All I ever wanted was a nice, quiet, settled-down life. I have been in a common-law relationship for seven years. At some appointed time, I will make her my wife. We love each other and for me, that's all that matters. We had a child together, a son, he's of my complexion and so very handsome. I said to myself, *I'm so glad I didn't use a condom.* The joy of being a father can't be compared to any other. The greatest accomplishment, up to this day I have no resentment.

The baby has my complexion but none of my attributes. I didn't raise an issue because I'm a happy father. I remained mute; I held my son in my arms and welcomed him into this world, I am so happy he isn't a girl.

I was at work when I got a call from home that the baby was in the hospital, and needed blood. My eyes flooded with tears. I was doing some dirty work, so my clothes were covered in mud. I rushed out and almost got hit by a truck, God is good to me, and it wasn't luck.

I got to the hospital. I asked my lady, "What happened?" It was a medical condition, and it required a blood trans - fusion. I'm willing and able when it comes to my son, that's my little man. I laid it all on the table; I'm ready, anything for my baby.

The doctor took my blood and tested it, to my surprise, it didn't match his. My jaw dropped, and my blood pressure topped. I loved and cared for this child! "How could you do this to me, Ann Marie? I'm up at nights with the baby; it's been a while now I haven't gone to work early. What have I done to deserve this kind of treatment?" She replied, "I cheated on you once with the neighbor, he promised to pay our rent." At that time you lost your job, we didn't have a cent. To get pregnant wasn't my intention; I was trying to prevent eviction. Ann Marie! I loved that boy, I can't believe this happening to me, and I thought you were the best thing ever happen to me.

I will never be the same.

THESE TEARS
TELL THEIR
OWN STORY

I feel misplaced. I'm a constant disgrace; tears find its rightful place on my face, a life of misery shows all over me. Tormented at work but even worse at home, there is no one to call my own. Voices in my head, saying I should end my life instead. I'm in so much pain but I still believe I have a purpose; sometimes life isn't clear to some of us.

In my life, I've experienced more tears than laughter, more anger than leisure and pleasure. I didn't have the luxury of love, to be kiss and hug. I feel worthless, maybe because I lack motivation, no one around me to hold my hand. When I think little of myself, I know I'm a failure before hearing it from someone else. Despite my low self-esteem, something in the core of my being saying, "I have a dream."

I am down, but I'm not out. When life grips me by the throat, in the pit of my stomach, there's still willpower to shout. My cries have access only to deaf ears, no one cares. I have lived in misery most of my years. No one takes the time to hear me out, so I do what I know best, I shut my mouth! I can't find my worth on this earth; people treated me as low as dirt.

The strangest thing about my hardship and loneliness, something inside me won't give up. I fall over and over, but it keeps lifting me up. I never could understand this core inner strength, I have been used and abused, but it remained scratch-free and without a dent. For a person who's going through so much, I marvel to see there's a part of me that remained untouched.

Maybe I do have a purpose, after all.

THEY SAY
TIME HEALS

I'm sorry for breaking your heart, I promise; I won't call you anymore because my very voice is tearing you apart. They say time heals, but I know you haven't done much healing, I can't explain the guilt I'm feeling. Both my bed and I missing you, sigh… you are not here, the future that we once planned is no longer clear.

I made the worst mistake of my life when I slept with your best friend. I thought you wouldn't find out but you did. Now I have only regrets to live with, you won't answer the phone, a voicemail saying you are not at home. I wrote a hundred letters to say I'm sorry, but I know you will never forgive me.

My ego got the best of me; I am not the man I used to be. Your best friend was walking around in her underwear when you were not here. I tried my best not to be tempted, but when I saw her half-naked, my body said, "You won't make it, Eve gave me the apple, and I took it."

I wish I could undo the hurt I caused; I wish I didn't harbor cheating thoughts. I have never seen myself as a man who would break your heart. I never thought I would be the one to make the tears start. You were my bright morning star, as far away the earth is from the sky, that's how far we are apart.

I had something good and I failed, if you should ever find another, please don't blame all males. I was weak and stupid, like a dog, I'm lying in my own vomit. I didn't deserve you, and I won't stop saying how sorry I am for what I put you through.

You were my backbone, my one and only love. The only one who says, "I love you," and make me cry, my ride or die.

THE SECURITY GUARD

My life is at risk while the boss man is home with his wife and kids. Working 18 hours a day to put food on my table, my baby mother says she's frustrated and unable. I'm trying to provide for my family, but my baby-mother constantly calling my phone, telling me she's lonely. Watching the boss's property to prevent trespassing, without knowing, a man is in my house both trespassing and partaking.

Invading my property without asking, lying down in her lap watching my flat-screen TV. I'm out here with a hungry belly dog by the name of Peewee. I have to walk with a flashlight, the place is dark, and I want to pee. Trying to make ends meet, while another man sweating up my sheets.

Trying my best to make an honest dollar, I didn't get enough education to be a white-collar. My baby mother doesn't understand the sacrifices I'm making and the risk I'm taking. She complaining about affection and attention but hear what! That can't buy the baby pram.

Why can't you get a regular 9-5? Baby! I tried; they need people with subjects and experience. Remember, both of us are high school dropouts and also young parents. Well, I need a man in the house, baby! Listen to me; get your body under control when you get aroused.

You are thinking about sex, and I'm thinking about success. Hear what! If you can't wait, find a date. I don't need problems, I need solutions. "Man you want," plenty in prison and the respectable ones in the army. Some well dressed, lazy ones in the police station.

You are too stressed; find a man who has time to invest for kiss and caress. The baby and my bills are my priority. Horny isn't salary. Pampers and milk have to buy, you want pleasure while the baby cries? I think it's best we say goodbye.

THE LOVE OF MY LIFE IN PRISON

I've sent many letters but no reply, I don't know what I would do if I should hear that he die. My baby doing time for an unsolved crime, the system treated him so unfair and unkind. No evidence, No defense on his side of the fence, my heart bled when I heard the verdict read.

Praying for him to come home, but my waiting seems in vain. Ten years now, and I'm here waiting just the same. I don't know how much longer I can wait, I'm human, and we sometimes lose faith. I just wish I could hold him in my arms again; I need my lover and my closest friend.

I need his arms to wrap around me at night, whispering words I'm longing to hear, but only to be reminded, that he's not here. I can't live the rest of my life like this. I can't keep longing for you; I can't spend the rest of my life like that's all I will ever do. My bed is cold and cruel, I'm weak and out, your love was my fuel.

The man I had planned to marry and exchange fluids with, to have kids—we were the dream team. It's hard to move on when you truly love someone. You are more than a day-to-day regular man. You were my life, my soon-to-be husband. God, have mercy on him, Protect his every limb.

The innocent man is behind bars, bearing the system's injustice scars. I wonder if I will see him again, my lover, my friend. I feel empty inside more and more as the years go by. I've no tears left to cry, my heaven-sent, I love you with all of me, and I know we were meant to be. You will always be the better part of me.

I love you baby, and I will always do. I can't wait on you anymore, and I know you would tell me not to. Baby, I'm a lonely woman who needs comfort; I can't live my life dwelling on the hurt. Please forgive me, and I'm sorry if I caused you any pain. The situation is driving me insane.

I'm sorry, my love.

ONE NIGHT STAND

I feel so good in your arms; I thought I meant something to you. The things that you make me do, Whooooo! The ways you hold me, and the words you told me, unfold me. The tender kiss and your hands on my hips, both our bodies head-on like two motorists. In a troubled world, baby, you have added the bliss.

I never thought I would be a one-night stand, but I would do it again. That one night was well spent, your flawless body and your scent, if I could turn back the hands of time, I would extend the length. The passionate love-making was so breathtaking. I was hoping, in your arms, I would be waking.

I always see myself to be conservative and a settled-down type of woman. I never thought I would be a one-night stand. I don't regret it though, please understand. I was longing for the touch of a man, but not by every man. Something about you weakened my stance, with you honey, there was no resistance.

I know I don't mean anything to you; I really don't want to talk on the phone. I am going to give you the address for my home. Just one more night of harmless fun, one last run and we're done. Your touch, my body is screaming for, I need more. I want you caress my 206 bones, make me your own. Your lips on mine will surely clear my mind.

I was looking out for you, but you didn't show. If I hadn't convinced myself that I'm a one-night stand, I know now. It hurt to feel like a woman without worth, I blamed myself and not the cat under my skirt. I feel awful, face to face with my reality, my choice was distasteful, and I feel horrible and dispensable.

All alone by myself, while you out there with someone else. The memory lingers like the touch of your fingers. Is one more night too much to ask for? Please answer me, baby.

THE HURT THAT YOU CAUSED

People say, you don't know what you got until it's gone. To be honest, that's simply not true because I'm not missing you. No longer reminisce on things that we used to do, the hurt that you caused somehow make me brand new. You didn't appreciate me; I'm no longer around for you to humiliate me. I'm proud to say, I'm not missing you.

It takes a bad woman for a man to recognize a good one. She's all that you weren't, I couldn't see through you, but she's transparent. All the lies shadowed the truth; everything that happened behind closed doors was on mute. You behaved like a lady in public, but you were a secret prostitute, I'm not missing you.

I have lived in the dark but in a new woman, I found the light. Sleepless nights telling myself things would be alright. Dreams that I wish I never dreamt, and words that were said, I wish I never meant. The pain I endured, I said to myself, I can't take it anymore. So many reasons to say I'm not missing you.

I was living a fairytale like Harry Potter, I never knew I was in bed with Delilah; the outcome was so astonishing that I lost for words and grammar. Moving on wasn't easy, but God's grace and mercy was the healing remedy. I was locking away myself, needed time to cry in my lonely corner. I couldn't face the world as another brokenhearted lover.

I was sleeping on a pillow of tears, wailing like a baby when I remember the years—trying my best to forget you. I never knew the day would come, I would say, I'm sorry I met you.

I am not missing you.

TO DREAM ALONE

What good is dreaming if I must dream alone? Man! You have a heart made of stone. The bigger the love, the bigger the heartbreak, Where's truth when I need it, for God's sake? You came in late at night, and silently taking your time, trying your best for me not to wake.

The passion and affection now belongs to another woman. You cut me deeper than any weapon, and I spend a lifetime waiting on the right time. Little did I know another woman was on your mind all this time? You played me for a fool, Sit on my feelings like a bar stool.

I wanted to turn back the hands of time, but the inevitable can't be reversed by a clock. I felt depressed and wack, the only thing left for me to do is sniff crack. Why? Baby, why! What did our relationship lack? I didn't refrain from giving you sex. Once you say the word, I'm already undressed.

You broke my faithful heart, tore it all apart and pushed it aside like an old donkey cart. A good man is hard to find, and those who are not already taken are on the borderline. I wash, cook and clean, try my best to be your perfect queen, but all my good deeds were in vain because all you do is complain.

I know how to treat a man, and still, I don't have one. Lying here in this lonely bed, you once occupied before I heard the word goodbye. I feel like a mascot without a costume, wish I could crawl back in my mother's womb. What am I living for if not for you? Who will I tell my troubles to? F**k the make-up and hairdo.

TWO BABY-MOTHERS SAME DRAMA

These two women are driving me crazy. They are comparing my babies, which one I care for more and who I adore. I feel like I walked through Hell's Gate when I met these two plagues. They dragged my name in the streets. They told my kids, "YOUR DADDY IS A DEAD BEAT." don't say his name, don't you ever repeat.

I can't live in peace, my mind never at ease. Their lives are miserable, and they wanted me to share the same fate. Daily, evil they pre-meditate. No matter how much I do for my kids, that's never enough. They told people that I don't show my kids love. My cup is full and running over, enough is enough.

They rang my phone, late at night. When I don't answer; nonstop disrespectful text messages to start a fight. Vexed and tormented when they can't get the chance to vent. They have me so paranoid and frustrated that I totally forgot to pay my rent. They used my children as scapegoats to get money from me. Two women I once loved are my two greatest enemies.

I love my children, but I regret the day I met their mothers. It sounds kind of awkward, but I'm sorry for the day they went in that labor ward. I can't be happy, and they make sure of that. They enjoyed causing me pain right around the clock. When will this nonsense stop?

I'm thinking about taking out a restraining order. Nicole and Junior, I know you don't expect this from your father. The both of your mothers are evoking anger. My first baby-mother was like; you are not minding your son. The other one is like, you will be in prison when I done! Oh please, give me a break for God's sake.

Both of them blocked me from talking to my children. Sometimes I wish I could go on a faraway journey like a pilgrim, I have so many questions to ask God, I need to talk to him. Lord, talk to me! When I prayed, all I hear is crickets. And water dripping from the faucet, will these two women cause me a premature death?

WHAT DO YOU MEAN?

When you say, "I love you," what do you mean? Do you mean you have accepted me with all my flaws? All I'm asking is, what do you mean? Do you mean through thick and thin you will be here? No crocodile tears. I just want to know before my true feelings start to show.

Jesus Christ, woman! What do you mean? Do you mean forever is eternity and not next week? Answer me! What do you mean? Are you going to remain loyal until the day you make a mistake and call me Devon instead of Donovan? Hold up your head and define what you just said.

When you say, "I love you," what do you honestly mean? Will you stick around because I can buy you the finest things in life? When I'm broke, will you be gone? Will I be out of your mind like I wasn't born? Let's talk. What do you mean when you say, I love you? Don't play dumb with me. Do you love me because I'm cute and fit to model with?

Wipe that look off your face. All I want to know is, when you say that you love me, what do you mean? Do you love me because I'm healthy now? But when I'm sick, you will be somewhere riding someone else's stick? I'm still waiting to hear what you mean. I'm not trying to create a scene.

Don't smile, I'm serious. What do you mean, when you say you love me? Am I your soul-mate because I'm in a good job and I'm easygoing? I can be taken home to meet your parents because I'm worth showing. Or maybe because I'm educated, I'm a gateway to get you elevated or being with someone of my class makes you feel motivated.

Don't bother with the crocodile tears. All I'm asking, what do you mean, when you say, you love me? She finally answered, "You are sexy and great in bed!" You feel so good that I can't get you out of my head.

Lmao

THE TRUTH IN THE WORLD OF LIES

I have to deal with lies all my life; tears aren't strangers to these eyes. The love that I'm looking for isn't in hand reach, deceitful women feeds on my good deeds like leech. Just to hear the words, I love you, from someone who actually means it. A chance to gaze in her beautiful eyes while she repeats it, true love isn't a secret. My heart has so many scars to show, like a soldier that went to battle. How much pain can one heart handle?

There was once a girl that I love so much. I used to feel like it was impossible to live without her touch. What changed all that? One night her phone rang, while she was sleeping, the name on the screen says Trevor. I answered, hello! The person says who's this, Tracy's brother? I said no, this is Tracy's lover. The phone hang-up in my ear, I said to myself, this girl thinks she's clever.

The next day we were having sex. She's like, oh God baby, you give the best sex ever. I said, yeah right! Did you say the same thing to Trevor? Where is this coming from? You know you are my only man! As far as I'm concerned, I'm one of many men. I'm not a crab, is like you giving me feces to swallow, make sure you leave this house the latest tomorrow.

That was the end of her story; all I want is one true love, not headache and agony. Just when I thought love run out on me, here's a beautiful girl in Walmart saying hi to me. She work as a merchandiser, didn't know I have a secret admirer. There waiting, no cashier by the cash register, she walked over, hi, I'm Jennifer.

Nice to meet you Jennifer, my name is Peter. I'm a little shy Peter, I know usually a lady don't do this, but my phone feels empty without your number in my contact list. No problem Jennifer, my number is 447-2636. Thank you Peter, you are such a life-saver, you are welcome Jennifer.

I singing, starting all over again is gonna be rough, so rough but we gonna make it.

TRUE LOVE CAN'T HIDE

True love has no hiding place. As you look at me, you can see it all over my face. My Sunflower, whenever you smile, my whole world is filled with laughter. Baby, you can't sweep true love under the carpet, Cupid smile the very first day we met. I feel blessed to be in your very presence, you have added value to my existence.

The best thing that ever happened to me is you. My dream came true, and I can't wait for the day you say, "I do." I lived and breathed for you. There's nothing I wouldn't do for you. I would move the sun and moon for the universe to see the star in you. My lady, your love lifted me so high, not even an eagle can reach where I flew.

I want to play with every string on your body like a guitar, Keep you wet like a reservoir. My touch is gentle—each kiss kindles, romance is the order of the night. Scented candles ignite, see-through lingerie excites my sight. Your sexy voice soothes, love songs are the icing for the mood, enjoy me while I'm being rude.

I kissed you on your forehead, thanking you for gracing my bed. I have a fire inside, burning for you, all the thoughts in my mind concerning you. Fortune and fame, you are all the riches one man can claim. I put my love in your hands. They say love is a risk in the wrong hands, but I'm willingly taking that chance.

I'm taking charge of my own destiny. Goddess, I need you next to me, my better half, and the best of me. My life, I would freely give for you to live. Baby, silver and gold, I have none, but I'm rich in love, I hope that's enough. Heaven and earth rejoiced when you say you love me, you put nothing above me. Hold me as if you rescued me from drowning; Keep me close and dear to you, my darling.

FLIRTING

No harm, no hurt, we just flirting and that's all. I will send text messages, no calls. Let me start by saying, I want to kiss your lips and caress your hips. I want my tongue to be in your mouth like a dental probe, call me your dentist. Keep you properly watered and blooming, like the process is photosynthesis. Have you rotating like the earth on the axis; study your body like an astronomer studying planets and galaxies.

Baby, you have a body that a super-model would die for, I have no reason to lie for. Your straight face, flat belly, perfect waist, my lips yearning for a taste. Thinking about you is the greatest thing my mind ever does, in my head like a brain tumor, I want to drive to your heart but I don't need Uber.

We just flirting, minimal risk……

Baby, I want to be all over you like salt on peanuts, I know you might be saying I'm bold and I've plenty guts. Angel, I'm all the man you will ever need, essential like the very oxygen you breathed. No harm, all in the name of flirting. Baby, I want to be closer than your shadow. I want to be in your thoughts, heart and tomorrow.

With you in my life, baby, I will be free like the sparrow, that would be the end of all my sorrows. Maybe I'm saying too much, but right now, I'm imagining your touch. I can't see you, but I can vision the blush. Baby, please delete all the messages I sent, OK. I know hussy is on his way. He has such little time; he's not around most of the time, most of all you are not in his time.

Sometimes I wonder if your husband cares as much as I do. He's always busy; he has no time for you. Sigh ... I just want to hold you and do all the things I promised to do, goodnight boo.

What kind of man would sacrifice a pot of gold?

YOU WILL NEVER KNOW

Everyone got something they had to leave behind. I love you with all of me, but you are not mine. I saw that ring on your finger, and it filled my heart with anger. Maybe I'm just jealous because I'm not your lover. I hate the fact someone else is in your arms, and it's not me, he's in the position I always wanted to be.

I have seen you walking with him and wish it was my hand you were holding. I envied every word you told him. Why do I feel he doesn't deserve you? Maybe I wish I were in his shoes, I would live to serve you. He's walking with you and watching other females, that's where he fails. You need a man who has eyes only for you, to cherish and adore you.

If I could just walk up to you and tell you how I feel. No disrespect to your man, but I'm just being real. If I grab your hand and ask you for a second, would that be sexual harassment? I'm a man who you can tell, "I love you," and I know exactly what that meant. A man who will make you feel like the only woman on this planet, your wish is my command, say the word and I'm on it.

Just a moment of your time in exchange for mine, I want to tell you words more than you are sexy and fine. Words like, "The sun rises and sets with you." Words like, "I would rather be in the desert with you than have rainy days without you." I watched you every day, but you don't even know I exist. I'm far from your mind like the mountain mist.

I envied that man for occupying the space in which I belong. I'm sure when he's making love to you, he's thinking of another woman. All I need is a chance to show you what *true love* is. Sometimes the right woman ends up with the wrong man, and the right man is someone no one pays attention to.

With me baby, it's all about you, there's nothing that I wouldn't do, to prove my love is true, I'm not Jesus but I would walk on the sea for you.

THE CHRISTIAN GIRL

She's been searching for that perfect man. No exceptions, he has to be a Christian, she's modest and seems to be a virtuous woman, searching in the church for that special one to be her husband. She searched the choir men, deacons and congregation to find that special someone.

I always admired her; I wish I could be part of her world, this sweet young girl. I watched her every Sunday morning, off to church, deep within me, I wanted to say something. I could feel the urge. If I could get a minute of her time, I might change from my sinful ways and give God my thanks and praise.

In my mind, she wouldn't look my way because I'm not her type. I like fancy clothes and jewelry, so she might think I'm all about the hype. Every Sunday morning, I would stand by my gate just to see her rushing to church. She doesn't want to be late.

She needs a man, not any man but the perfect one, how can I be that one? I know she is lonely, and I saw the frustration. Even in the church, she couldn't find a compatible man. Sigh … and I'm far from being the one. I love the party life, and I'm not ready to be a Christian. But who knows? Maybe one day I might make that right and final decision.

I can't let a good thing go to waste. Sunday I am going to church because for all I know, I might be that person. God knows the reason. She's passing by, "Wait on me! I'm going in the same direction. Hi! My name is Rayon."

She replied, "My name is Susan." "It is so nice to meet you Susan"

Hands clapping, she's so beautiful and throughout the entire preaching, her I watching. Songs of praise, I looking towards better days, in the church I'm smiling from ear to ear, look like a clown but I don't care.

WOUNDED
HEART

All my life, I have been searching for love in the wrong places: constantly falling for pretty faces. The beauty and the sexy shape, the ass, only I know the pain it all caused. My eyes fall for what they saw, and my heart suffers the consequences because of my eyes negligence.

The smooth skin, the bright wide grin, the sweet soothing words; I can't even tell when these girls are lying. Blinded by what I can see, but their true intentions were all about how to hurt me. I'm lost in their beauty, but they find their way in my pockets, these beautiful pickpockets.

They are beautiful, but their personality stinks. They like the flashy lifestyle, the money and blings. None of them love me. They all love things, I'm just another fling, and I know this by the way they thinks. Nails and Brazilian hair are all they care about. When I said, I care about you; it is like nonsense coming out my mouth.

I'm fooled by their beautiful faces, and naïve to their ways. The hell they put me through, I wish it on no man. Believe me, for everything I say is true, If I knew what I know now, I wouldn't be this blue. They say love doesn't pay the bills, but what they don't know, fast life kills.

Women are beautiful like roses but be mindful of the thorns, you have been warned. I'm easy to fall in love, I suffered many broken hearts. I'm always seeking a new start, willing to forgive and turn another page to hide the rage. Just by believing everyone isn't the same, if I'm wrong, I'm the one to be blamed.

The sleepless nights I'm asking you to avoid. When your heart is broken, nothing can fill that void. They say love unconditionally, but I say love with conditions, for your sanity is your only stance. Without your sanity in a relationship, you will lose your balance. Think! Stay far from ignorance.

You can be foolish when it comes to romance, but be wise when it comes to who you love. Know when you have been taken for granted. Know when enough is enough, know that invitation is different from an insult. Your every step determines the end result.

LOVE QUADRANT

One love but I shared it equally, "Angel" I will never do anything to mash up your family. I'm here to take the hurt away and show you a brighter day. Let me softly kiss your lips to help you forget about yesterday. When I'm done with you, the sun and moon will envy you my star, People will be able to see your happiness from afar.

One love, but all parties are pleased. My wife is a happy woman, and my side chick can't get enough of me. I'm the man who comes along when everything in your life is going wrong, baby take my hand. Rest your head on my shoulder, I'm your comforter. I will never forsake you like your ungrateful worthless lover.

I'm not a magician but I create magic, let me massage your body and relieve the tension in your pelvis, put an end to your mid-life crisis. Baby, all your man do is hurt you, but I'm here to nurture, nurse and add pleasure. I'm the man who knows how to fulfill, women's every need and demands. You deserve love, and I have love in abundance to give. If he makes you feel like you are dead, with me, baby it is time to live.

I know one question roaming in your mind. How is it possible for me to love and please all these women? Baby, I have all the time, love and affection to give, my passionate love will give you a renew reason to live. Your peace of mind starts here; I'm more than words let me show you how much I care. Baby, have dinner with me in Milan. Let me treat you like a high-maintenance woman.

I'm a gentleman in every way, not a regular guy who's day-to-day. I'm a cut above the rest because I have all the qualities that others don't possess. It's not self-praise, I am not just the best but the greatest. They're plenty of fishes in the ocean, but I chose you for salvation. Let me lead you to the "Promised Land."

You're Not Going Anywhere?

L ife is journey of mysteries. "Endurance" is the gas on this journey; hardships are hurdles you must jump over. "Envious people" are potholes, avoid them! Decisions are stepping stones. "Mistakes" are eye openers; "Failure" is just being human. "A day" is another chance to make it right; "Relationship" is risking your sanity, not all recover from its toxicity.

"Loyalty" is like a past story, once upon time. "Faith and confidence" are nothing without each other; keep them closer than a brother. "Circumstances" are trials for proving how wise or how foolish you are. "Happiness" is a state of mind; it has nothing to do with money, what it is? It's the serenity with one's self. "Peace and success" are both attainable, depending on the energy you attracts in your daily life.

"Friend" is a sarcastic word, totally the opposite in meaning. "Enemy" is an ambiguous word, it will put you in a confused state of mind because the lacking of transparency. "Money" is like intimate relationships, it comes and goes. "Naysayers" are people with fabricated expectations of how your life will or should turn out.

"Victory" starts when you acknowledge what your purpose is. "Who you are," That totally depends on your deeds not what you achieved. "Family" is another F-word, you will learn more about that along the way. "Death and life are neighbors," life has plenty promises but death ways are sure.

"The graveyard" is the richest place on earth, it is here that you will find all hopes and dreams that were never fulfilled, inventions that never seen, books that never written, the hit song that never heard of. Your deeds talk louder than your money, what you stand for in this life will shape your afterlife.

THE LONELY POLICEMAN

I'm in these streets fighting crime when I should be in your presence spending time. I'm trying my best to serve and protect, while in my bed, I left my most valuable asset. Empty promises on the phone each night, and I continued to reassuring you that everything would be alright. Yet I'm out of sight.

Late nights patrolling, firmly gripped my gun, but I wish, at this late hour, you were the one I was holding. To serve and protect, I vowed to the government, but my personal life is filled with broken promises. I always see myself by your side but my true colors can't hide.

Busy being a crime fighter and forgot totally how to be a lover. "My life is at risk," repeats over and over in my head like a scratched disc. My woman no longer has faith in me. I'm not the man I'm supposed to be. "I'm sorry" are words of little significance when my love life is imbalance

Trying to get rid of guns and cocaine, crack, little did I know that my lady was dating, behind my back! I'm upset, but I can't be mad at her for that hideous act. My time is spent among the deceased and the scum on these streets. I pray he's a better man than me, and he knows how to treat a lady.

I do love you, and I do care, but I can't sit back and watch law-abiding citizens living in fear. I'm sorry, my dear, and I wish I could catch all your fallen tears. The life I live makes me a man with little or no love to give. You don't deserve the hurt.

Forgive me, baby.

THE LADY IN THE BAR

She sat all by herself looking sad and misplaced, I noticed tears was trickling down her face. I stared without her knowing, on her face; the years of pain were showing. I can't sit any longer and watch. I walked over and asked, what's wrong?

She said, "You talking to me?"

I replied, "Yes, I am."

She said, "I hate men."

"Why do you hate men?"

"All men do is used me. I thought I was beautiful, but I guess not because they all refused me." She put a whole bottle of vodka to her head with eyes blood red. "Please stop!" She's still drinking … gulp, gulp. I had to wrestle her for the bottle. "You don't need a drink, you need someone to talk to, and I'm here."

She said, "No one cares."

"I do care, and I'm all ears, wipe your tears." She's sobbing; I leaned over and gave her a hug. "My advice is all I have to offer, and I hope it will help you to conquer."

"A man respects a woman who respects herself. What you're doing now, only will cause even more damage to yourself. If I was seeking a mate, my first pick would definitely be someone else. Don't drown your sorrows in the bottle. Be sober so you can pursue a better tomorrow. A man admires a strong woman.

"A woman, who puts out her best, even when everything is going wrong, will one day find the right man. Never use the wrong man to define all men. That person in the mirror has flaws too, so examine you."

She said, "That's true."

Knowing what a man wants is different from knowing what he needs. A man is the head of the household, but, in the end a woman leads.

I HAVE A CRUSH ON MY PROFESSOR

My intentions are clear. He's teaching but not one word I hear. In his beautiful brown eyes, I dazedly stared. He's well-groomed and wears a sensual perfume, when he speaks, I get so weak. Only if he knew I'm his to keep. If I tell him how I feel, he will think I'm offering sex for good grades, which might lead to a tirade.

I once heard he's not married, but he's in a relationship. He doesn't talk about his life much. He keeps his business tight-lipped. I sit and imagine a chemistry that's never been taught in his class. If he only knew my thoughts, he would stop teach chemistry and start to teach culinary arts. Thinking about tasting his bold lips, suddenly he shouts my name, Katherine! Stand and tell the class the answer to the question, "What are lipids?"

I stand up, feeling a bit stupid. Everyone turned around and looked at me, expecting something lucid. I stood there, rocking nervously and saying to myself, *I was sitting there thinking about him, and he chose to humiliate me.* I said, "I'm sorry, Professor. I didn't hear you clearly because this girl who's sitting next to me is chewing a piece of gum loudly.

The professor said, "I hope you're not telling such a lie so boldly."

"No, professor."

"OK, what's the last thing you heard?"

"Hmm, professor, can you please start over?"

"Get out of my class! You are a time-waster."

"Professor, please give me another chance!"

"I'm sorry, I can't."

I walked out with my head held down like a wilting plant. I can't tell my parents what transpired here today. If I am going to lie, I have to lie all the way.

My mom noticed I had overslept. "Catherine, wake up! What happened? Are you not going to class?"

"Mom, someone in the class has the Coronavirus, so the professor told us class will be cancelled today."

"So, when will you be going back?"

"I really can't say exactly."

"I will call the professor."

"Mom, he says he will send emails. He no longer uses that number."

"Strange!"

THE DISTANCE IN OUR RELATIONSHIP IN 2020

Gazing at your beauty and admiring your sexy body, bite my lips while I reminisce. The sad thing about it, I only can see you on a video call. I'm surrounded by four walls. I'm in my bed alone at night; my pillows are the only thing I am holding tight. Miles apart, but you are always in my heart. The pain of missing you hurt so bad, I don't know when I will see you again, and that makes me so sad.

The most hurtful thing is to be in love with someone that you can't hold near. I wish you were here. When I'm down and you are not around, to hug me and erase my frown, I have to turn to my phone. The love we have for each other are so great, and that's why we're holding on to faith. Because of circumstances, we are miles apart from each other. Our love stands the test of time and makes it through the roughest weather.

But to be honest, I'm lonely at times, and I need my lover. Your arms were my shelter; your sweet angelic voice in my ears was my comforter. To journey this lonely life without companionship, that's even a painful thought to start with. Even my body parts missing you: my lips missing your lips, my hands asking for another chance to romance hips. My eyes miss gazing upon your beauty from sunset to sunrise. When will I see you again, my lover and my best friend?

Life is too short to live alone. I don't need anyone but you in my home. To hear or see you, I have to pick up my phone. How long will I be living like this? No companionship, no hug, no kiss. This distance only brings pain, borders are closed. I can't leave out on a ship or a plane. I feel like I'm going insane, I never saw this coming, unbearable strain to both body and brain. How will we make it out of this? I don't know how, but I know for sure. I need you here and now!

Waiting on the borders to be reopened

THE GIRL
IN MY CLASS

I can't focus in class; this new girl took over my thoughts. I gazed at her each time she passed. My teacher noticed something strange going on with me, it's like I'm in a trance. She told me to stand and read what's on the board aloud to the class. I stood there mumbling, look what this girl caused, standing there looking lost. I feel so embarrassed; I had to apologize for not paying attention and for not being keen to every word that was mentioned.

I went home that evening thinking about her. I'm sorry for the fact I was embarrassed by the teacher in front of her. She's been on my mind from the very moment I laid eyes on her, so beautiful like polished jasper. I go to school for an education, but I have to admit, she will be a distraction.

Another day at school, I promised myself I would focus this time, writing down the notes from the board. I glimpsed at her because I felt a little bored. She's not just beautiful but also very intelligent, a first-class student. She doesn't even look in my direction, sigh…. I crave her attention.

Academically, my grades are below average, and my parents did their best to build up my courage. Here I'm thinking about a girl who's thinking about maintaining her grades. My mom and dad work so hard on the farm to send me to school, and I don't want to be a disgrace.

I began to study more frequently because a dunce—well, that's not me. I'm up late at night studying, trying to be the very best I can be. Standing and answering questions in class that's how she noticed me. Now I'm doing well. My mind isn't on her anymore, what the hell?

Now I know how it feels to be in her shoes. When you make it to the top, what's below isn't of your concern.

WHY DO
I CRY?

I cry because I'm poor, how can I say I'm safe and secure when my needs have been ignored. Mr. Politician! You talking about the places where we live, the landfill lifestyle, remember you make it what it is. I need love and acceptance but you shunned me and called me a nuisance. I'm willing to work but no one willing to give me a job. So I end up with no alternative but to kill and rob. I have no skill and stealing and killing isn't my will.

Why do I cry?

Poverty lowers my self-esteem and eating away my dreams. Sometimes, I'm sorry for the day I was born. People looked down on me with shame and scorn. I cry because I'm poor, what I called bed, you call garbage; you passed me in the dump, eating an expired Vienna sausage. I don't feel like a human being, all my life I feel like something from out the Amazon, wild and mean.

Why do I cry?

I can't believe suicide on my mind, life been treating me so unkind, I decided this is the end of the line. I'm tired of praying and fed up of trying, to be alive is a waste of my time. If I'm gone, I won't be missed; I've never been hug or kiss. I don't know what love is, I heard it before on a music disc. I always wonder if it is something on a grocery list. Some people's lives have all the colors like a rainbow, but my life has only one color. Blue, that's my everyday hue.

Why do I cry?

I wish life would be better but it won't, I even once prayed to be in your shoes. Why live when I've nothing to give, I grew up among scavengers like myself, I know no relative. My faith fades away like yesterday and my heart no longer look towards a brighter day. My tears represent my melt down, no smiles to erase by frown; happiness is a part of me I've never seen, because it never shows. Don't feel sorry for me! Do me a favor, help others like me.

TURNED MY NEGATIVE INTO A POSITIVE

I got pregnant at age 16 and fell out of school. Some say I'm the illiterate fool. My parents put me out; nothing good about me, coming out of people's mouths. My baby-father says the baby is not his. I got involved in the go-go dancer biz. I have to provide for my baby by any means necessary. I will show my baby boy that he doesn't need a father to be somebody.

Dance my butt off to buy the baby pram. I might not be someone's ideal woman, but what people thinks of me won't alter my ambition. I will do anything to provide for my child. Pride doesn't put food on the table, and it surely didn't pay for cable. My life didn't turn out how I expected it to be, but I won't let this reality become my destiny.

I want my son to get a better education than I did. No one

knows the depression I struggled with. I put out my best on that stage, but what they can't see, is the rage, a young single mother without the help of neither family nor my child's father. I tell myself I can do this, held my head high because it's my life, and I'm the protagonist.

The years have passed. My son is now 14, and he's doing well in his class. No help from anyone, but I have proven to be a strong woman. When I dance and collected money, I save for my son's education. He might not like what I do for a living, but he can surely say, "My mom is my superwoman." I still make the time to help him with his assignments, provide for him and make sure I pay the rent.

My son's teacher calls me; she says my son is now the top boy in the entire school. Yes! It is obvious he follows my golden rule. I told my son, in whatever you do; try your best to be number one. In this information age, the key is education, never give up, and say yes I can. That's my golden rule; I'm so elated, thanks for this great news. I learned in life, success comes by what you stand for and not necessarily by what you choose.

The greatest choice I made in my life, I believed in me no matter what the circumstances may be.

THE SON OF
A CRIMINAL

My father was a murderer; I'm the son of a predator. I'm sad to say my father's life was taken by a licensed firearm holder, I look like him, but we are not the same. Because of him, I lived a life of misery and shame. Only God can forgive him for all that he did, I'm innocent and yet his sins I have to live with.

I don't have a criminal record, but people treated me like a criminal. Everywhere I go, people see me as my father, the animal. If I could only afford plastic surgery, I would do it tomorrow bright and early. I'm fed up with this life, and I don't know how long I will survive. Because of his past terrors my days are numbered.

My father didn't care about my future. He's dead, and I'm left here to suffer for the sins of a dead murderer. This face and his surname bring me excruciating pain. I'm afraid to get my girlfriend pregnant because I don't want my child to live like a peasant or a nuisance. Trying to be a law abiding citizen but I'm stereotype and naturally disliked.

God! I'm so stressed out right now. I want to live a clean, pure life, married and go to church with my wife. No one wants to give me a chance. They all live in my father's remembrance; I just need an opportunity to fulfill my plans. But how can I prove myself without acceptance?

I can't walk on the street without watching my back. I needed a haircut and stopped by the barbershop, but everyone walked out. They all went to another shop, the barber told me I killing the only livelihood that he got. I can't live like this, I'm going to talk to my girlfriend tonight, we are moving to Memphis.

THE SOLDIER WHO WENT TO WAR

My son went to war for five years and never returned. Right now, that's my biggest concern—no letter, neither a word from the American government. I'm living in torment and resentment. The day before he left, I begged him not to go, and he still went.

So many lives have been lost in the war in Afghanistan, both Americans and innocent civilians. A suicide bomber knows nothing about love. They believe in killing a large number for their honor. Each night before I go to bed, I send up a special prayer for all the American soldiers.

My son always wanted to become a soldier, but the career path I chose for him was a teacher. But he had made up his mind, so I said, ok "Fine!" I so wish he had a change of heart back then. I wouldn't be here carrying this burden; I can't focus and can't sleep because I'm too heartbroken.

I pray and hope for the day I will see you again, just to hug you and cherish every moment spent in your presence. The house feels empty without you, there's no essence. There's a pain in my chest that never rests. Only God knows how I feel, I wish I didn't have to go through this ordeal.

Sitting on my balcony, watching another day goes by, these eyes of mine has no more tears left to cry. I heard a knocking. "Must be them damn kids?" I'm going to warn their parents about this constant bothering. I'm too stressed for this "Bull**it!" These kids are too provoking.

I opened the door, my son had returned home. Thank you Lord! My prayers didn't fall on deaf ears; they are finally answered after all these years. I hugged him so tight and thank God he's alright.

"I'm overwhelmed with joy, son, welcome home!"

THE ONE LIFE
I COULDN'T
SAVE

I've been a doctor for 25 years. I have saved many lives, but one life I couldn't save was that of my husband. He had colon cancer. He was a great husband and father to our daughter, I used to sit by his bedside and cry with him. I have plenty work to do, but I took time out to lie with him.

The hardest thing was to watch him suffer; the man I once saw forever with, my soul mate, and a perfect match made by Cupid. Groaning in excruciating pain, I heard him softly called my name. I held his hand and said, "I'm here, and I'm not going anywhere."

His physical feature has changed. He lost plenty of weight, and his face no longer looks like the man I once called my mate. Although I knew he would not make it, I told our 10-year-old daughter that her daddy will be OK. A lie I wished I didn't have to tell, that same lie might one day take me to hell.

It's hard to watch him like this. In pain, he clenches his fist, and I'm standing there helpless and hopeless. "My lover, I will miss your arms around me at night, the tender kiss, the man who brings me true bliss." I'm a doctor, but there's nothing I could do to help alleviate his every agony.

Although it saddens me that he died, I'm glad God put him out of his misery. I'm now a single mother without words to express to my 10-year-old daughter. What can I say to mend her broken heart? Where and how do I start? Her dad used to reads her bedtime stories. He will surely be missed.

I will never love again. I lost my husband, lover and best friend. Watching my daughter grow up without a father will be the most devastating encounter. Watching her cry is so heartbreaking. I'm now a widow in search of a better tomorrow. I hope to see you again my hero.

THE CHILD
BY THE
WINDOW

B y the window, looking out for her daddy to come home, but "Daddy" is nowhere in sight. "Daddy" was hit by a stray bullet while standing at a stoplight. The child waited patiently and, out of curiosity, she turned to her mom and said, "Mom, daddy used to come home early?"

Her mom replied, "Maybe he's working late. Just have a little faith. He will be home before eight."

"OK, great."

She waited, and still, there was no sign of him. Mom got worried because this isn't like him. She dialed his number, and it rang without answer. She started to wonder, *what could have possibly gone wrong?* She paced back and forth in the house, what could possibly happen to my spouse? Her eyes filled with tears, the little girl asked, "What happened to Daddy, Mommy?"

"I don't know, Sally."

At 9:30 p.m. the phone rang, "Hello!"

"This is Dr. Williams; I'm calling from City Hall Hospital. Is this Catherine?"

"Yes"

"We found your information in your spouse's wallet. He's here at the City Hall Hospital, his condition is critical; he was hit by a stray bullet, which lodged in his vertebral canal. Hello! Catherine, are you there?"

"This can't be happening! Are you sure this is the right number you dialed?"

"I know this news is hard to absorb. I'm sorry to be the one to convey such a horrible ordeal, but we have to face it because it's real."

Catherine and her daughter rushed out of the house to catch a cab to the hospital. Catherine said to herself, *everything about this situation is abysmal.* They both got to the hospital, and Catherine introduced herself.

The doctor said, "Your spouse was critical, but now he's stable." As to whether he will walk again, he will be unable." Oh my God! Catherine began to cry uncontrollably, loud screams echoed throughout the lobby.

Her daughter, Sally, consoled her: "Daddy will walk again, Mommy."

"We are not sure about that, Sally."

Sally replied, "You always told me to have faith, Mommy. How come you don't have any?"

"You are right, Sally, and I'm sorry."

They went by his bedside, hugged him and squeezed him tight. They cried together, She gently whispered, "I will never leave you, my lover."

STILLBIRTH

Years ago, but it still feels like yesterday. The memory is a constant reminder each day. We called you Jeremy. That's the name your dad chose when he rubbed my belly. He was so happy that we were having a baby. Your daddy was the happiest man alive. His smile was so bright, and every night he would kiss my belly goodnight.

Both of us were elated and excited. We couldn't wait for you to enter this world! He wanted a boy, and I wanted a girl. We were preparing your room, although you were in the womb, hoping and praying to see you soon. We couldn't wait to hold you in our hands, the opportunity to give parenthood a chance. I can't wait to see your pretty little face and give you a warm embrace.

At 21 weeks pregnant, I went for an ultrasound. Your daddy jumped when he heard the result. He was overwhelmed with joy that I'm carrying his son. Being pregnant, I felt extremely loved. He didn't let me lift heavy stuff, and he stopped me at times and said, "That's enough!" Your daddy bought everything in blue. Little did we know that we would lose you?

At 36 weeks, I noticed I didn't feel you kicking. The place was so silent I could hear the clock ticking. We called Dr. Williams, who instructed me to head to San Diego's Mercy Hospital for a stress test. My eyes were wetter than a rainforest. Your dad arrived at the hospital breathless. I did another ultrasound and I couldn't find the courage to look on the screen. The doctor showed me the screen, with no sound and no movement seen.

How can something so wonderful turn out so horrible, so fast? In my thoughts, that's the question I asked. The doctor hugged me. We all cried together. The doctor called it, fetal loss, ten years has passed but up to this day I lived in the past.

WHEN MY FATHER DIED

When my father died, I felt so empty inside, no more tears left to cry, I have lost my hero, the man who taught everything that I know. My role model and fine example, I lived to emulate him, sorry you are not here to see your grand children, Jerry and Kim.

Jerry looks like you, Kim learning to ride her first bike, daddy I miss you and this life going to be a lonely journey without you. You taught me how to be a gentleman, now I'm not just a family man; I also married a wonderful woman, her name is Joan.

Daddy I hoped I become the man you wanted me to become, I hope you proud of your son. Daddy, if tears could bring you back, you would be here, I cry you a river because you are the world greatest father. The love you shows my mother, is the same love, I show my wife, my son and daughter.

Daddy you missed my wedding and you also missed out on meeting your grand children. Miss out on my achievements; I bought a house without borrowing a cent, finally stop paying rent. Daddy, you taught me to be independent, learn to stand as a man on my own two feet, put out effort for ends to meet.

You were a great dad and husband to my mother, nothing feels the same anymore. I watched my mother cried by the window while the rain pours. Never know I would see a day like this one, standing over your grave with a bouquet of flowers in my hands.

Daddy, nobody missed you more than my mom, you was her rock and shoulder to lean on. Her peace of mind, I can't say or do anything to stop her from crying. I can't put a smile on her face; it's not possible for anyone to take your place. Rest in peace until we meet again my father and best-friend, your time on earth came to a premature end.

MY LAST WORDS

O n my death bed, so much is going through my head. If I get a second chance to live my life over, would I do things differently? Would I still save money for the age when I become elderly? Would I save millions of dollars knowing it can't save me? Would I marry the same lady, although she forsakes me?

So much going through my head in my final hour, would I still fire a man for reaching work late and hinder him from putting food on his family's plate? All these questions might kill me even faster, but I need answers. Would I still pay my employees minimum wage and carry the lump sum to my grave?

When I look over my life, I was a cruel man. I marvel at the fact I lived this long. If I got another chance to make it right, would I still be selfish and boastful? Would I still be that greedy boss man who always wants more, even when his cup is full?

My tears drowning me in this death bed, so much weight is on my head: why I chose now to acknowledge my flaws and all the people I hurt for what I thought was a worthy cause. Lord, make my death bed my confession portal. Today might be my last day in this hospital.

Forgive me for the suffering I caused. Sorry to all whom suffered from job loss and salary cuts. I know you all hated my guts. I'm the sorriest man alive. If it were up to me alone, I would end my life. I never knew I had done so much wrong until I got bound to this bed of damnation.

Lord, my last words are, "Forgive me for all whom I have hurt. Give them the peace within themselves to forgive me, as well. Thank you and I hope there's air condition in hell."

MY HUSBAND GAVE ME AIDS

Being a stay-at-home wife was the best decision I have ever made to please my husband. I kiss him good morning and prepare his breakfast before he even asks. I have his clothes pressed and ready for work, matching tie with his favorite shirt. I tried my best to treat him well because I know a good man's worth.

I kissed him before he leaves the house, letting him feel the core of my love; I hoped my love is more than enough. While he's away, I do chores all day, make sure the house is clean, and smelling great when he steps in. I live for this man; I believe in our union, for our future, God has a plan.

When he reaches home, we sit and talk about how his day went. It's mostly OK, but sometimes he just needs the space to vent. His dinner is always prepared whenever he gets out of the shower. I tried my best to be the perfect wife and lover, honest and loyal forever.

I don't deprive my husband of sex. I'm here to please, whenever, wherever, however, he pleases. I'm the all-in-one woman, the only woman he will ever needs. Anything else is greed. My precious treasure, pleasing you with the best of my ability, is my pleasure.

I woke up this morning with him on my mind, but I noticed he's not feeling well. He didn't get out of bed, and I didn't compel. I thought I could nurse him but shortly after he suffered a seizure. I called the ambulance immediately because I figured he needed to see a doctor.

He's admitted to the hospital. One of the doctors called me and said she has bad news, but keeps it confidential. The doctor told me he has AIDS.

I said, "What? Go and do another blood test!"

She said, "Mom, the test is accurate, and you might have it too, which is so unfortunate."

Oh my God, why me?

MY AUTISTIC SON

As a mother, it's the most painful sight to watch your child suffers. Struggling with a disease there is no cure for. Not smiling when I smiled at him, always rocking. Sometimes his hands flapping and the same phrase he constantly repeating. I can't send him to a regular school, so I got him a tutor. Although his illness will be with him for the rest of his life, I wanted him to have a bright future.

His father isn't around much because he's embarrassed by him. He is my child, and I will always care for him and I will always be here for him. He's not the ideal child that any parent would plan for, but his illness only makes me love him more. His father doesn't even take time out to play with him, wouldn't even take the opportunity to teach him about the Bible and pray with him.

I have to work twice as hard to see about my child. I'm so exhausted and haven't relaxed in a while. I wish my husband would help out, but it seems we are on our own. What's the sense of having a good-for-nothing man in my home? He can't see eye to eye with his own child that his sperm helps to create. I don't know if this is shame or hate. He said that he loves me, you can't love me and you don't love our child. It seems his Unconditional love comes with conditions.

I didn't carry you for nine months to abandon you. You are a part of me, and I will never leave you. Your father neglected us, but your mom got us. Your disease isn't a limitation but a greater push to go beyond. Your situation makes it easier for me to make your father my ex-husband. We only need each other. We don't need that useless man.

Love you world without end, my son and best friend. You are my asset, not my problem!

MY ABUSIVE FATHER

My best friend's dad would come home drunk, and beat his wife like it was for fun. Beat her senselessly, and ripped off her nightgown. At the age of six, Tom was the eyewitness to his father's wickedness. All he could do was cry because he was helpless, he watched his mom sit and cried relentlessly, stressed and depressed.

When his dad is sober, he would hug her and say how sorry he was, but that means nothing because tonight is a repeat of the same thing. Plenty times Tom would run to her rescue, but he would kick him and asked him, if he wanted to beat too? She had scars all over, the work of an abusive father.

He was the only child and was too young to do anything, Tom says, the screams were deafening and being an eyewitness of it all was threatening. Her eyes are red and her body had cuts all over, what a demon he has for a father. His mother did everything to make him happy, and all his father does is treating her like a jalopy.

She prayed that he would change but that far from being arranged, the man was unchangeable and terrible. He didn't know what God was waiting on to answer his mother's prayers, maybe until he kills her. He asked, when will this end! The pain and brutality that she endures, Tom says she's the strongest woman he knows and that's for sure.

The strangest thing happened one day; while he was cursing tom's mom, he had a heart attack. They didn't get the chance to call the ambulance. He died on the spot. Tom says, he guesses God work in a mysterious way, although that wasn't the result for which his mom prayed. Tom says, he feels God removed him permanently, maybe it is better that way, he finally saw his mom smiled! For the first time in a long while, he says it was the most beautiful smile.

MY MOTHER'S BRUTAL STORIES

My mother told me her life story, a story I wish I didn't hear, a story of abuse and great despair. It's a story about my half-brother's dad. He was an abusive man. He hit her with a champagne bottle and broke her hand. He pushed her out the house in middle of the night, with a broken hand and her clothes by her side.

Her story was killing me slowly, I'm sorry she told me. Imagining the pain she went through bring tears to my eyes, sitting there listen to her tearful story have me stagnated like am paralyzed. A life of abuse and taken advantage of, she went through so much that it's hard for her to find the peace to laugh. The hurt was just too much for her to identify her true worth.

The ordeal she suffers, I wish on no women. She told me a story of her older brother, he was very cruel to her, and how he had her toting water from a distant river. One day, she fell with a bucket of water, what remains in the bucket he used to throw on her. Overworked her like a slave, a life of pain shows on her face like it something that's engraved.

Her stories evoke emotions I didn't know I had. Just listen to the excruciating pain she went through gets me so mad. She told me a story of her mother and father, her mother died when she was very young. Her father raised her, but his life didn't prolong, he was murdered by a man who he always gave a helping hand.

Her dad was a good man, but the day he failed to help a person who always in need, is the last day that he breathed. My mother fell out of school, but she wasn't a fool. Neither family nor friend gives a helping hand, but she pushed on because her tears are a language that only God can understand.

PANDEMIC

Borders closed, the love of my life, my future wife, I don't know when I will see her again. She's in Maryland, and I'm in the Caribbean. Things are not getting better, the news only delivers terror. Millions are infected, and thousands are dying each hour. Businesses closed. People got laid off. What am I going to do without my better half?

Vaccine trials failed. Our bright future together looks pale. Hear the pain in your voice over the phone. When will we be together in our own home? Depressed and alone, a video call can't replace your physical presence. We ran out of words to say, the awkward silence, the sigh, we are both feeling a bit tense.

No announced date for reopening. The borders remain closed, your arms around me at this time I needed most. I can't stop the tears from falling; I refused to answer the phone when you are calling. I don't want you to hear me crying, deep inside, I'm dying. You asked me if I'm OK, I said yes, but only God knows I cried all day.

If we knew this pandemic was coming, we would have cherished every moment we spent together. The kisses would be longer, and the hold would be tighter. I wouldn't let you go, my beautiful flower. I wrote these words in tears, for the years we lost out on and a future we can't press fast forward on.

If I never see you again, I just want you to know. I love you, world without end, my lover and my best friend. The chance of a lifetime was to spend my life with you, but now I don't know if I can live without you. All my life, you I needed to be in my life. There's always some kind of blockage, but the love we have strengthens our courage.

Some people take their loved ones for granted, and they are still more fortunate than us. They still have each other. The love we have for each other can't be compare to any other, but we are not sure if we will ever be together. It is hard to love someone and can't be with them, even harder when you can't find a solution for the problem. Sigh ... I wonder how it will end.

I will forever love you.

ORPHAN

Everybody says I'm ugly, I guess that's why my parents abandoned me. I don't know why my mother didn't think of abortion, maybe she did but it was a tough decision. I know an orphanage isn't the best place for me but I'm a child without a family. People came every day to adopt a child, but no one thought of me, not even to show me love for a little while.

The orphanage is the only home I know. I've no other place to go. I woke up each morning and feel like I'm not worth seeing. I feel unloved and neglected, my parents left me on the pavement at age seven and now I'm eleven. I try to smile at times to keep the pain hidden but it's such a heavy burden.

The other kids make fun of me because of my big eyes. They watched me and made funny noises. All I need in this world is a sense of belonging. I'm sick and tired of feeling unwanted and love-starved, in this life, all I want is my fair share and it doesn't have to be a whole half. I just need to be hold and be treated like a human being, why you all treated me so mean?

I woke up this morning with tears in my eyes. A lady walked in, she noticed l looked sad, and asked, "What's the matter?" I told her my life story, and she said, "No child should suffer in such a manner." She whispered, "I'm going to take you home with me." Someone finally looked past my appearance; this was a great feeling of acceptance.

The feeling is unexplainable — a place to call home where I'm comfortable, a mother figure around me to make me feel consolable, and a playground to play like a normal child. Living is now worthwhile, I hadn't smile in a long time but now I'm smiling all the time.

I'm now grateful for life; my foster parent showed me all the love I ever needed. It makes me so excited; I never thought I would ever get accepted! I've been rejected all my life, my "Good Samaritan" finally arrived.

LANDFILL
AND MY WILL

I have lived in the landfill all of my life, I know nowhere else. The vulture filled skies, the flies, the environment which smells. My running water comes from the drain or whenever it rains, just a summary of my life of pain.

I didn't ask to come into this world. I can't believe I'm searching the garbage for an expired cheese curls. I can't wait to see the garbage truck, just to see if I have any luck. The landfill provides for me, it gives me a salary and a meal whenever I'm hungry. The government does nothing for me.

There's nothing to hold on to, only my will to survive. A landfill is a disgusting place, but it keeps me alive. I sell expired stuff that companies throws away; that's what gave me a payday. No one cares about people like me, even when I said hi, they watched me with scorn because of my scanty attire, and my scent high.

No one expects anything good from the slum. They call us hooligans and scavengers, and we don't even exist to some. I didn't have the chance of getting a proper education. I didn't have the chance to enjoy the luxury of belonging to someone. I am not even sure if I'm human.

The inhumane treatment and resentment towards me are so extreme that it kills my self-esteem. I'm someone without a dream. To be honest, I'm afraid to die. I am not sure if there's any milk and honey beyond that sky. The government is talking about the places where we live, they said, we are worthless and to society and we have nothing to give.

We are good people in a bad situation; we are the unfortunate and the easy to forget. There is greatness embedded in us but there's neither place nor space for us. I wonder if God put me on earth to suffer. I doubt my purpose is to dwell in this gutter. Show me a sign or might as well take my life because this isn't living.

LIFE BEATING

I had my fair share of disappointments and struggles; I have been beaten down by the evil deeds of people. Betrayed, misused and abused, giving my love to the wrong people is one of many reasons why life is teaching me a lesson. Trusting people is the worst thing I ever did to myself; unfaithfulness and dishonesty makes it even harder for me to love someone else.

I'm wrestling in my sleep with the nightmares, which are trying to overthrow my dreams. I woke up in tears with no shoulder to neither lean on nor console me. My whole life, I'm my own enemy, too caring. Now I'm the one in my lonely bed crying and staring. I thought I could give my love and live happily ever after, didn't know being a good person would make me suffer.

Everyone mistreated my love, now I know for sure I had enough. Being a good man taught me one thing: being stupid isn't an option. Live to please people is like trying to start a truck with an empty tank, with no diesel. I thought my life would turn out beautiful by my good deeds, I guess I was wrong, or maybe I followed destructive leads.

Bearing the pain and squeezing my fist tight, I'm living but that doesn't mean I'm alive. The dead rest in peace but not even in my sleep I can rest with ease. I'm tormented in my head and restless in my bed. I can't do anything right in this life: the struggles, the deception and strife.

A beautiful smile doesn't mean I'm happy, and have a little money doesn't mean I'm wealthy. Don't be fooled by the appearance of things but the absence of things. The money and rings can't tell what's going on deep within. Not everyone gets a new beginning, many losers only dream of winning.

I've trusted many with my heart, and they all ripped it apart. It simply means they used and refused me. To Journey this life alone with no one to call my own, what are fame and fortune if I have no one around or in my home? Through it all, I still believe someone is out there for me. For me to live alone, I doubt that's how my life is destined to be.

All I do is cry behind this smile.

LIFE OF A MIGRANT

My country has neither job nor opportunities for me; I decided to seek a better life overseas in order to provide for my family. I didn't feel welcomed at all. I got poor customer service both at the airport and the mall. When I speak, my accent turns heads; the prejudice and racism toward migrants were so widespread.

I got a job that is paying me below minimum wage. Deep inside, I'm disappointed and filled with rage. My co-workers called me an outsider; I have been ill-treated by my supervisors. They cursed me daily and belittled me. They shout at me, whenever I passed, they push up their mouths at me.

My family thinks all is well, what they didn't know, I was living in hell. They have no idea that I sleep in my work clothes at night, my skin were covered with mosquitoes bite. The apartment I was renting, look like an abandoned building. I can see the stars through my ceiling, on my door termites were feeding.

I've left my country with visions of something better, but an unexpected twist, I've suffered beyond measure. I didn't know I'm hypertensive until I came here. I'm so stressed that my head began to show a lot of gray hair. The inhumane conditions that I'm undergoing, was so mind blowing. My family calls for money but how I earned it? That's a painful fact they all unknowing.

The grass isn't always greener on the other side. Many people hide what they are going through because of their pride. All my money goes into paying bills. I can't save; I say to myself, this country is planning on sending me to an early grave.

I don't know how I will return, the money for a plane ticket will take years of savings, and so little I earn. I dreamt of a better life, but I guess that dream is a nightmare in this part of the world. Not even wishful thinking can survive here, better is somewhere but surely not here.

A WIDOW'S LETTER

I never thought I would see the day you are not here by my side. The pain I feel inside no longer can hide. I can't hold back the tears; you have been so good to me over the years. You have created a world of love, you make me know "what is love," and it felt so good that I couldn't get enough.

I'm alone in this big house. Our eldest son moved out with his spouse. All my strength is gone, and sometimes I feel like I'm just too tired to keep going on. The memory of us haunts my mind, my sunflower; our love was one of a kind. I never get tired of hearing I love you time after time; I don't know when I will stop the crying.

All I have are pictures of us together, the happy memories still lingers but the pain of your death is way greater. I am standing by your grave, watching the petals falling from the bouquet of flowers that my tears showered. My tears washed your grave clean. This can't be real; it has to be a dream.

The days felt longer than usual, and the nights are extremely cold and brutal. Both life and time angers me. Loneliness and emptiness conquered me, how will I live without you? You were the only true love I ever knew. Forever, my lover and soul mate, I thought getting old together and dying together was our fate.

Death is inevitable, and still, I can't accept the fact that you are no longer here. I can't hold back the tears when I remember the 50 wonderful years. We were such a perfect pair. My king, your queen will always love and miss you. Sit by my doorstep and reminisced on our years of unforgettable bliss.

I am up listening to the quiet of the night. The loud beat of my heart reminds me that I'm still alive, but I don't want to be. I am depressed and drained by the grief and agony. It's hard to keep up when I lost the only man that I ever loved.

BARREN WOMAN

Everyone around me has a family. My boyfriend made up his mind to leave me if I can't give him a baby. I love kids, but I'm unable to have any. Even one would be enough; my boyfriend says our relationship is not only based on love. He needs a child, and he's not seeing it happening with me. It is a hard decision, but if I'm unable to have a baby, he will have to leave me.

I've been to the gynecologist and got fertility pills, I doubt being barren is God's will. My neighbors watched me with pity in their eyes. They knew me for years, and I guess they must be wondering what's going on between my thighs. My relationship is on the line, while People have my business on their minds. God! Where are you at this time?

I noticed my boyfriend has a frown on his face more often, I know the reason is because I'm barren. He doesn't kiss me goodnight anymore. Sometimes he got off the bed.

to sleep on the floor. It pains my heart to know I might never be able to give him a child, he looks so sad; He hasn't smile in a while.

I have been taking the pills and nothing, the doctor told me to increase dosage. I did and few months later, I went to the bathroom and I've noticed I was passing a lot of blood. I was experiencing a miscarriage. I screamed! And my boyfriend ran to the bathroom. He called an ambulance; we have gotten a swift response.

The ambulance came, I wasn't feeling any pain. My boyfriend held my hand. Tears in his eyes, he got a little emotional on our way to the hospital. When I got there, doctors rushed with me, I was bleeding heavily. I lost my first baby. Doctors told me I had to stay until the pregnancy tissue has passed. "Lord, I have so many questions to ask."

"Doctor, I have been trying so long, and now I think I lost the only one."

"Why do you say that?" I explained my situation. The doctor said, "did you know if your spouse has a low sperm count, it can also put you in this very same position?"

No, I didn't know. "Well you know now," I said to myself. He was planning on leaving me when maybe he's the one who can't give me a baby.

BITTER BABY MOTHER

We had a child together but because the lack of trust and loyalty, we no longer a happy family. She told my son, "Your father is careless and he's worthless." He doesn't care about you; I'm the one who's here for you. Poison my son's mind against me, trying to turn my own child into my enemy.

She hates me so much. She said that I'm dead to her; people would have thought I cheated on her. She has cheated multiple times behind my back, and hates me for finding out the facts. She doesn't let my child call me, she prays for all types of evil to befall me. She hates the very sight of me, maybe if I die, that would make her happy.

I did all I can for my son, but that doesn't stop her from saying I'm a worthless father. The hate and anger are like unto no other. I tried my best to give him a proper education, but his mother isn't grateful for my contribution. She told my child, "Your father doesn't love you." I'm the one you see when you're in need, he puts everything above you.

My child doesn't know his dad's birthday, and he doesn't call me on Father's Day. His mother says, "I'm dead to her anyway." She dragged my name in the streets, I can't have any peace. I have moved on with my life, and she's jealous of my newfound wife. What does this woman want from me?

This woman adds more misery than the plagues of Egypt. She has turned my life into a horror film like *Tales from the Crypt*. She's jealous of the way I'm happy without her. She put out all the effort to see me hurt. I don't know for what reason does it worth, but this woman lives for my discomfort.

I hope my son will realize one day that his father loves him endlessly. Don't blame me for his mother's mistake; it's a burden I'm unwilling to take.

BLIND AND UNLOVED

I s there someone out there for me? Someone who will love me for me? Will they be able to put away the fact, I can't see? All I need is my place in this world, just to be hold and called someone's girl. I need someone to be there when I wake up in the morning, to kiss me on the forehead and say, "I love you, my darling."

All the guys passed me by and don't even bothered to say hi. I feel unwanted, and I wanted to die. No more tears left in these unseeing eyes to cry, no need to try. My life is filled with discrimination and frustration. My cane is my only navigation when no one wants to help a lonely blind woman.

I was born blind and for this reason, the world treated me so unkind. No peace of mind, I find. My life is all miserable and dark; although I was born blind, I can't get accustomed to the dark. I'm still fearful whenever I go for a walk. The

noise of the busy street and the sun's unbearable heat —
through it all my willpower guides my feet.

There is no one around to console me. Words like I love
you, no one ever told me. I felt like I'm no one's child, and
I can't seem to get the amusement to smile. I've never been
touched, never had the privilege of compliments to make
me blush. My every day is another painful journey. Why
me?

I hope to get married and have children someday, but it
seems no one is coming my way. Living my life like every
minute is the last, and I no longer give thanks for each day
that had passed. No joy in my life, what is the sense of being
alive?

I'm hopeless and stressed most of the time, but I don't show
it. I put on a fake countenance, and no one knows it. If you
walked a mile in my shoes, my life would mean hell to you,
but it's more like a curse or spell to me. I need someone, and
I need love. Is that too much to ask for?

DIVORCE IS THE HARDEST WORD TO SAY

This marriage not working out, half of the time, I can't figure out what we are arguing about. Maybe we get too complacent, I'm not telling you that you are beautiful and you believe because I'm a man, I could go on without compliments. No breakfast in bed, I had to get up and toast my own bread. You no longer massage my shoulders, I stopped buying you flowers.

You totally forgot my birthday, walked passed me like it's just another day. I can't find the words to make you smile; lately you look mean and it takes nothing for you to get hostile. You turned your back in bed; it seems like you regret the very day we were wed. The words I love you, no longer in our vocabulary, we no longer thinks it's necessary.

I have work in the morning, I had to set alarm to wake me up, when you rise in the morning, you bath and put on your make-up. When I came home from work, I have to cook my own dinner; you home all day watching Jerry Springer. You eating all my groceries, and left only Ramen Noodles for me, do I look like a Chiney!

I rather live alone than live in a dysfunctional home, passwords on our phones, both our faces wearing a frown. Two years now we haven't had sex, when I see your mean face, I said to myself, abstinence makes sense. You dressed like an old woman in the house; you look like Casper the friendly ghost.

We don't ask each other, how was your day? We just go on our merry way. Where's the spark we once had? How we end up so bitter, lonely and sad? So many questions but there are only one answer. Divorce is the cure for this cancer, she's fed up of me and I fed up of her, we are two miserable humans.

I know if I ask her for a divorce it won't be a problem, the only problem here, is being together. I now reached home from work, she's going church in the morning, she busy pressing a skirt. Can I have a minute of your time? What you want? Speak your mind! Ok, I'm asking for a divorce? She replied, no problem, of course, I was going to ask you but I'm glad you asked me first.

Thank you Jesus!

FAIRYTALE

My years and time wasted and all the different flavors I tasted, can't compare to the bitterness you added to my life. I called you my queen. I see you as my wife, yet you cheated and trampled my pride. Your arms were once a place under which I abide, I can't believe you cheated and lied.

All the skeletons in your closet could full a graveyard. So much you did behind my back while I was working abroad. I cried when the truth was revealed, you stepped on my heart with your spike heel. My heart is in so many pieces, I doubt time will ever heal. I thought I found something true, didn't know I was living a lie, only God understands the tears that I cry.

I love you so much that I would try to put out the sun with a single touch. You ruined me, and I was too blind to see what you were doing to me. We had a child together; I thought that would mean something. I was checking around for the perfect engagement ring, you were behind my back doing your thing.

Loving Delilah is loving pain. I gave you all my sanity, and now I'm running insane. You said because you were lonely, you cheated on me. You hurt a man who's working hard to provide for his family. We weren't meant to be, and it is even clearer to see. Maybe you were just part of my journey, and all you had to offer, is your body.

I cry a river till it forms an ocean. I did everything right, I wonder how I ended up with the wrong woman. The agony is unbearable, and your actions are unacceptable. What did I do to deserve this? I cry till I can't recognize myself, I looked in the mirror and my reflection look like someone else. I feel like a mantis that got run over by a motorist.

My nights are like a vacation in hell! Your voice is so annoying, I can't believe all this time with my heart you were toying. You are wrong, but you're going down fighting. Lord Jesus, please deliver me from this before I do the wrong thing. They say karma is a bitch! But, for some reason, I feel life served me the wrong dish.

ABOUT THE
AUTHOR

Donovan Broderick is a Poet/Writer based in Kingston Jamaica, throughout his years of writing poetry/stories; he had develops his own style of writing. He won several poetry contests and got published in both local newspaper and international, UK Teen Magazine. He's a gifted writer, based on the fact that all of his write ups touched the inner part of its reader. All of his topics evoke emotions. His work kept the reader engaged and every word is a lesson, that's what makes his style of poetry writing more gravitating. His innate skills are unmatched and anyone who reads his work will see the art of a new era of poetry

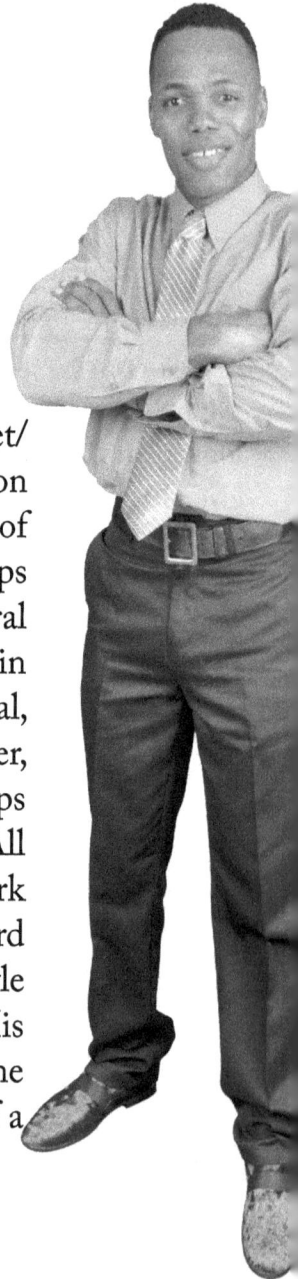